Farewell and Toodle-oo

Poems

Michael J. Cahill

MARY
LUISA
PRESS

FIRST EDITION
6 April 2024
Published in the United States by Mary Luisa Press

Typset in Garamond
Cover design by Farnicle Tweed
ISBN 979-8-224-50975-1

www.maryluisapress.com

For my parents and family who keep egging me on

Contents

Hurry, hurry, life is waiting—
Not to begin, but for you to join in.

G.F. *Armazetto*

ONE

Fetch

Not all breeds can be trackers,
especially this one with his
diminished olfactory sense
one ten-thousandth that of mine.

When he thinks he's clever,
palming the thing he pretends to fling,
I still dutifully sprint into
the nothingness of its direction.

Where… where…?

It only takes a backward glance to see
yet again, behind his grin,
the faintest flash of guilt.
And still I bounce back in earnest, as I always do.

Because the real game is differentiating
between betrayal and play,
knowing that lasting love
can well withstand an act of misdirection.

Two Old Friends

She was hunched way over
like the small letter c,
unable to defy
the concentric circle of herself.

It seemed
were she ever to trip
she would not be able to fall
but only roll,

lopsidedly falooping
end over end
in an off-centered,
slow and steady rotation,

easily, laughingly,
loping down the lane,
humming a heady "whee!"
with every circumference.

With his greatcoat and pipe
he was larger than she,
also bent over
but like a capital G,

curled into himself,
an anxiously wound watch
puffing along
tight by her side,

ever hand in hand
to keep her from rolling away.
Or to keep, perhaps,
from being left behind.

Other People's Children

Emerging from our solitude
and coming into a clearing
not far from the park,

I didn't notice the sun had come out
until we were shadowed
by the hover of a child's kite,

its winged blue translucence
dancing there on the path in front of us.
As we glanced up to see what it was,

a haze seemed to rob you
of the light in your eyes
and locked you up quick.

Just like that you shook yourself
free of it with a wince,
the kind that accompanies

the ripping away of a bandage.
Summoning such warmth and perseverance,
you threw me that merciful smile.

The courage it took for you to make music
of so many happy cries floating up
over the trees and down to us.

Long Journey Home

January is the worst month to miss the bus.
Book bag too heavy, coat too thin,
sky so grim, clouds bruised and swollen.

No give to the asphalt in this bitter wind,
not like in summer when the pavement
is softer and a less cruel shade of grime.

The cold burns my face, numbs my fingers,
needles through my leather lace ups
biting my soles, stinging my toes.

And still nowhere close to the misery
of treading this long hour home
over ash gray patches of ice,

late for dinner, no time
for homework and chores,
behind again as always.

Will next year not be here soon enough,
when my teen years arrive and, at long last,
I am confident, cool and smart?

Willful

Yes, I have fallen
many a time.
And every time
I am up again
because I do not
agree with gravity's
naive presumption
that it knows better
than love.

Slow Reader

My sloth-like reading,
a target of ridicule in my youth,
has turned out much to my benefit.

A book for me now is a warm invitation,
drawing me in, not at speed but at ease.
Pouring slowly as I do

over each word, each re-turning
of a well turned phrase, I am struck
by the unquickness of its creation,

the measured craft called upon
to create it, as would a sculptor
extracting form from mass.

I'm entranced by the cautious tread of any
who would enter such a quarry,
chipping into the rough rock of language

to bring forth a fiery figure
from an alphabet of cold unspoken stone.
How can I do any less

than to approximate the pace at which
such carefully considered words
have been fashioned just for me?

Teapot

Squat dutiful soldier and cheery companion,
my reliable Brown Betty,
generous in its gleaming girth
seeing me through these many years,
trusty little teardrop
warming so much more than a heart.

How I learned the hard way what a mortal sin
it is to scrub that tender inner belly
when a light rinse is much preferred,
doing one's utmost to protect
its delicate encrustation, improved with patience
and seasoned in increments from years
of steeping in leaves of Ceylon.

With every black and amber pour,
every steamy cup of comfort,
I am taken back to the fastidious days of my naïveté
when I shocked you with my ignorance.
Surely the innocent sacrilege of scouring yours clean
cannot have been the only reason you left.

Piracy

This happy afternoon a friend, his children and I
fashioned pirate hats from newspaper, a pastime
of silliness taking me back to my own childhood,

to a kingdom devoid of care or consequence,
to a place of raucous adventure born of
imagination, safety scissors, paper and paste.

All was well until a six-year-old cornered me
with cardboard sword and eyes flashing of conquest,
when my heart knuckled up into a fist of stone.

Freebooting no longer seemed a game as
inches above my assailant's victorious brow
glowered the spectre of her three-cornered hat.

On the frontward face of it,
in a mocking plume of business-section text,
was my primary stock investment—zeroed out.

Before this day I would not have believed
the guttural shriek of a grown man's terror could be
drowned out by the giddy gales of a little girl's laughter.

Grandfather

I have missed meeting you, knowing you.
I have only scraps of your pleasant nature
and comradely ways, fragments
of who you may have been to my father
sifted from conversations with him,
the ghost of whomever it is
that feeds the deep and gentle invocations
that regularly well up inside of him.
For so long now I've gathered
breadcrumbs of you in the little ways
he moves and speaks and reaches and stands
and strolls and laughs and sits and mourns,
imagining how the two of you differed—
that he never smoked despite the many
photos of you with cigarette or pipe in hand—
or traits you both may have shared
such as that always reliable smile.
He is older now and has changed so much
from when my questions first began.
He lets me hold his hand these days
and that is when I get to meet you.

The Slumber of Aspens

Reaching and straining
high into November,
finally free of their bright seasonal clothes

they dance on tiptoe
in prayerful extension
from wiry root to uppermost limb,

patiently waiting
that I might look away
so they can wriggle their fingers,

beseeching the sky
to let drift down their nightshirts
and robe them in white.

TWO

Blessed Thievery

I'd have never believed
that taking a picture
could steal a piece of one's soul

until after you'd gone,
when I happened upon
an image that ended up taking its toll.

Customs

So as not to rumple or wrinkle,
I lay with care all that I wear
layer upon layer
in a case for my suits—
my suitcase.

With full intent to carry with ease,
I bundle together all that matters,
adding and adding with cautious
consideration to my bags—
my baggage.

With the slipping in of so much minutiae,
I consolidate a tight and tidy congregation
of so many worldly concerns,
of briefs that are anything but brief—
my brief case.

Every thing onto which I cling
and which, in return, clings faithfully to me,
is built up and bundled, leveraged and layered,
packed deep and much in need of truncation—
my trunk.

The weight of all that should travel well,
an accumulation of my many wants,
however impractical, I press them in
and lug, lug, lug them along—
my luggage.

That everything is lost in transit
turns out not to be the devastation I anticipate.
I am deaf to apologies, which hold no sway.
The surprise of my smile has washed away—
my grief

with relief.
And at customs I have nothing to declare.

School Closures

My eyes struggle open to a morning too brilliant
as though the sun, no longer sky bound,
spills up into my room from the yard below.

Out my frosted window from two stories above,
our garden, like magic, renewed overnight,
re-blossomed in gossamer,

billowy, thick and bright.
I scramble down barefoot, tug open the door
to a crystalline symphony, hushed and white.

Across the way a neighbor knee-deep
spades a path through a blinding desert
to where our street used to be.

Something We Ran Over

"What was that, Uncle Ted?"

With a nonchalant flick of his cigarette
and a husky sigh of smoke
he mumbled into the mirror—
"Either a lumpy doormat or a very flat dog."

My little sister cried all afternoon.

First Flight

*"What could this atmosphere possibly mind if
a spec like me may ruffle its fragile perimeter?"*
(Brother G.F. Armazetto)

The year is 1503 and clear as day
I picture a modest monk,
Brother Gianluca Fausto Armazetto,
shipwright and sail smith.
He keenly observes a harbored boat afire,
the roiling heat billowing its sails with such force
as to almost lift the craft from its moorings.

Thus inspired, he experiments
with fabric of every kind
until happening upon silk, which,
when stitched into an open ended sphere
and filled with hot air,
rises high on its own to the heavens
carrying with it a basket of many heavy stones.

Emerging from months of seclusion,
on a clear Spring day the good Brother
summons his village to witness
a grand surprise, a dazzling teardrop tapestry
of silk and science borne aloft
in a delicate defiance of gravity.

So artful a feat of ingenuity
no human had beheld—
the earth as viewed from some distance above,
a dumbstruck crowd of two hundred below—
concluding with the gentle monk's
graceful declination into a deafening
throng of squeals, shouts and screams.

All smiles and pride throughout,
Brother Gianluca had not anticipated
so explosive a reception.
As the glorious contraption lightly touches down,
he is rushed by the frenzied crowd
who carry him on their shoulders
and convey him to a nearby pyre

where he is flung into the conflagration
and burned as a devil.
The monstrosity of his satanic handiwork
is ripped to shreds in a frenzy of rage
and tossed on the fire after him—
its ashes drenched in holy water and vinegar,
the earth salted so nothing in this place will grow.

Some 200 years pass before
two French brothers of no particular faith invent
the second hot air balloon—calling it of course, the first.

Penitence

I turned on my lights
and pulled in behind
a funeral procession today.

Not a terrible way
to latch onto a police escort
and run some red lights.

But the couple in the back
of the car in front of me
had their heads together

as though in anguish.
And I found myself,
out of respect,

staying with the procession
all the way
to the cemetery.

Timepiece

The watch I keep is a sentimental piece,
once possessed by my father
who inherited it from his.

It's a heavy gold pocket edition
that stopped cold in 1948,
never to be wound again,

only to be held from time to time
to feel the weight of one father's
immense regard for another.

Sunday Best

When I was a boy presentation of self was entirely
a matter of manners, especially so on Sunday—
hair combed, tie cleanly knotted, suit sharply pressed,
shoes all a-glimmer, posture impeccable.

In a family of ten we'd often worship in shifts and,
shuttled off on my own to early service,
I'd amble the three blocks east
down Mahantongo Street to St. Patrick's church.

It was obligation, not imperative, that drove me there
way back when the mass was still in Latin and,
after yet another week of parochial school,
I hadn't the humor for one more liturgy.

Every so often, though not often enough, at the very
last moment my feet would dodge me away
from that gothic edifice and carry me farther on down
to Centre Street where all the stores were closed.

I'd amble with solitary ease, a figure of leisure,
as though indifferent to this threadbare little town.
The affectation of a grown up stride almost fueled
the impression that the manners were paying off.

And for what—the tiny thrill of a ten-year-old
blatantly blowing off God,
of gawking with guile into unlit storefronts,
of ticking away one interminably gray hour

until I could return home under the guise
of one who'd been suitably sermonized—
despite not a single break in the crease of his trousers,
as though one might have spent any time on his knees.

Supposition

Even though his voice
is already really, really high,
I sometimes think
if my cat were to inhale helium,
his voice would become so high
that only dogs could hear it.

Season's End

It never fails that I am utterly thrilled
by the amber, plum, and blood red
flurries of Autumn,

newly gathered in drifts like snow,
the fluttery offspring of red oak,
sugar maple, sassafras and dogwood

all feathering about my feet
as I stroll, and even skip like a child,
kicking with great big leg swings

at tufts and mounds and bundles of leaves,
swirling them up into flight again
and all the while wishing,

as my own winter approaches,
that I too may improve
to shades more radiant

than those of my youth—
that my own downward drifting
might inspire others to raise me up

for one more lovely flourish,
showing off how I was
most dazzlingly brilliant at my last.

THREE

An Extravagance of Apples

A road stand bushel basket,
nestled like a new family member
in the back most seat of our station wagon
between my brother and me.

Having won the appointment
of guarding this latest family treasure,
we each shoulder up to
its flimsy poplar-strip weave.

Holding back its bright, rosy
stained glass bounty, we lean close
to breathe in the cool steam
of that crisp leafy scent.

Our sisters strain in their seats,
twisting around to verify
the best apples are not
being pilfered by the boys.

Farewell and Toodle-oo

Miniver Berkley-Beeche, though quietly
reserved in private life, is handsomely
laid out in full three-ring regalia—
pastel plaid silks, clown-white base,
Raggedy Ann cheeks, frilly saffron wig
and four-inch rubber nose.

Mini-Bee the Clown, as she was billed,
is on full display in a luminous
metallic lemon yellow casket that
would be appropriate to her four-foot-four stature
were it not for the pair of bright blue
patent leather oxfords (size 18 double-E)
protruding through the coffin's end plate.

Making every effort to be a great big
banana split of a funeral, colorful, bountiful,
bright bouquets of helium-filled balloon animals—
Mini-Bee's specialty—clutter up the chapel.

The organist grinds out "Bringing in the Sheaves"
accompanied much to her annoyance
by slide whistle, bass drum and bicycle horn.

And after all the water-squirting lapel daisies,
hand buzzers and bubble guns have ceased,
after the chorus of Whoopee cushions has faded,
(for the most part, anyway)
we are brought to a final moment of quiet regard.

Mini Bee, in her lifetime, delighted a great many
and was dearly beloved by multitudes.
In this instant we observe as one body
the true depth of the laughter that has left us.
It's a remarkable sight—levity in repose.

The only wailing now is that of
two soggy souls down front,
a couple unaccepting of their daughter's choice in life.
And, in a way, that's funny too.
Though in all fairness it may also have been a bit much
for them that so many of the mourners
were seen to arrive in just one car.

Out for the Evening

There we stood all in a row
awaiting our goodnights as the two of them,
smart and beautiful, ran down the line of us.

So sorry to leave, but so happy to go,
she pressed in warmly to each one,
familiar and present and bountiful as snow.
Protecting her lips, she planted the sound
but not the kiss and was off in a mist of magnolia.

Then down he'd swoop with that growl of affection,
terse lips and a smack of stubble,
dealt with speed like a hand of poker
and not even time enough to be
anxious for my turn—then gone,

as though he'd never been there at all
but for a whisper of Old Spice and spearmint
clinging to the warmth he'd left behind.

Inconvertible

I envy my brother
who looks so good with facial hair,
like a movie star, villain or hero,
Mustache, goatee, slight or full beard,

whatever the configuration,
he wears it so well.
Whereas I, in my many attempts,
end up spotty, sparse and scruffy.

After several weeks
of one particularly earnest endeavor,
my daughter innocently remarked,
"Dad—you look like a cop who lost his job."

And that was it.
The only convincer I ever needed.
These many years this face has remained
naked, clean and accessory free.

Though I still envy my brother,
donning any variety
of well-whiskered personalities.
Becoming someone else at will.

Next to the Funeral Home

The parking lot
with room for half the city
is barren of cars.
Not a vehicle in sight.

A passing dog walker stops,
the taut leash causing her little gray terrier
to turn and look back.
The terrier relieves himself.

His master studies the expanse of asphalt,
its rows and rows of empty spaces,
glances from cemetery on the right
to mortuary on the left.

With a cock of the head
and a moment to mull it over,
she offers a gesture of agreement
to the sign at the entrance that declares:
  Customer Parking Only

Note to Self

This, dear friend, is no lament,
whatever one's age or firm intent,
whether newly found or recalled from the past,
for however long it decides to last—
all love is young love.

Lullaby

Because of the intangible nature of music
I cannot say with certainty I have never been sung to.
Though denied the gift of hearing since birth,
I do wonder every day what music must be like.

As a child I was lulled by other things—
tender fingers through my hair,
a bit of rhythmic rocking, the plush of a toy at bed,
none of which soothed my senses.

What little I know beyond its tantalizing
thrum and quake is that music speaks
through my hair and skin, to my organs and bones,
to a life subtracted of timbre and tone

in waves of rhythmic incantations
that will never truly reach my other senses
or embrace my soul as it has the depths of others.
I have seen singers move their mouths with longing,

players romance their instruments
with passion expressive and uncontained
and not at all dissimilar to acts of love.
But I cannot say for certain it was ever meant for me.

Though once, perhaps, so long ago,
while cradled close, a soothing sensation
vibrated softly through my skin—
tender, rhythmic, intimate, and just to me.

Could that have been a lullaby?

Twilight

Childhood is reborn in me
with summer's sacred reverie.
It's miracle of sunset skies,
all shooting stars and fireflies.

Arrivals / Departures

A hard lacquered bench
thick with many coats of green paint,
yet suitable enough for reading.
I wait.

A slight figure,
valise in hand,
eases up the ramp to the trains,
holds an overcoat too warm for this climate.

Stops half way.
Two full minutes.
Frozen. Frail.
Turns, lost.

Moves to nearest bench.
Sets down valise and coat.
Almost next to me.
Sits.

Half turns.
As if to speak.
Then withers.
Sobs.

Quietly.
No wish to disturb.
None to take notice.
Travelers come and go.

Shaking now.
Sniffles into a cuff,
fumbles
through overcoat pockets.

Grateful my father
encouraged me
to carry one,
I produce a handkerchief.

Brief hesitation.
Takes it.
As fingers brush mine,
it can no longer be helped.

Head drops to my shoulder.
Hand clutches my sleeve.
Weeping now.
With great need.

All in silence.
No wish to disturb.
I deflect passing interest
with a pleasant nod.

No one will disturb.
The shudders diminish.
A straightening up,
correct again.

A tentative pat of fingers
unruffles my sleeve.
Uncertain of being heard,
I whisper a consolation.

"Hey, brother!"
My sister rambles down the Arrivals ramp,
hubby close at hand
lugging bags.

I push through a fresh flood of travelers
to trade an embrace.
Just that fast,
the figure, valise and overcoat are gone.

Half way to the parking lot
I remember my book
and trot back to the lacquered bench.
Where it sits squarely perched.

On top, my handkerchief.
Folded.
Neatly.
Soaked through.

Sainthood

Does it have to be sanctioned by the church to be official?
There must be so many unrecognized saints,
certainly more than history could recount.
Flightless angels who gave their all
for the betterment of others.
How forgotten they must feel,
purveyors of great kindness
with names unrecalled,
unprayed to.

Though perhaps they are grateful to be unobliged
to altar and pillar—no height from which to fall—
instead, rather relieved to be set free
on the open sea of anonymity,
adrift in their willingness
to be small.

FOUR

A Winter's Day, 1960

Looking out from the warmth of our kitchen
I see my mother, a willowy fresh faced Florida girl
in the thick of her first northern weather,
brooming a foot of new snow from the roof of our car.
Across from her my father in suit, tie, coat and gloves,

working a long handled ice scraper like an oar,
addressing the windows in earnest and
grimacing back at a bounce of morning sun,
the calves of his trousers ballooned out from the tops
of his shiny black five-buckle Liberty overboots.

Once he's gone and she's huddled over a hot mug
about to begin her own busy day,
I slip out to where they'd worked on the car together,
mesmerized, not by the rectangle of dry pavement,
but their footfalls in the snow around it.

Wanting to add my own impression, I lift a tiny boot.
But I cannot disturb the lacework of her doe-like treading
among the sun-sparkled craters of his great big Liberty's
and imagine a day when I too would be just as grown up
and heroic and beloved for simply going to work.

Lessons from the Tree of Knowledge

Behind the gates of the priory
where the priests from our school lived
was an orchard of apples—
two sloping acres of billowy trees
heavy with fat, fleshy fruit
that would otherwise go to rot.
Once a year in our tiny coal mining town
we were bussed to this sanctuary,

where at any other time we'd be unwelcome.
Tiptoeing from the ground and
teetering atop unsteady ladders,
we plucked from those ruddy boughs
so many McIntosh freckled in rose and amber,
topping off baskets and baskets
bound for the crushing mill.

Weeks later, when returned to us as cider,
we'd peddle it to our families.
No one cared that much for cider
in those weighty, unwieldy glass jugs,
but the time-entrenched tradition
that made our parents buy it
was the same power that compelled us
to pick the apples.

The same apples the older boys
would sneak in and steal throughout the season.
The same apples the priests,
from behind their dark windows,
would see us stealing but never bother to stop us.
And then I'd remember that they too were boys once
and perhaps the guilt would always be familiar.

Scarred

When I have been wounded,
either slight or deep,
my instincts push me to a private place.
Solitude always feels right
for coming to grips with an assault.

Healing is another matter altogether.
Especially when the skin has closed over
but the offense continues to fester.
Sometimes a scar is so reviled
it takes on another persona altogether.

I know a young woman who was once a cutter
but concealed her scars with tattoos of uplifting images.
Now when she looks at her wrists
there is no hostile reminder but rather inspiration.
And that has made all the difference.

Like welds on a machine,
The places we repair ourselves
become our strongest tissue—
fragility and durability
in symbiosis.

Beyond any savagery that opens us up,
a tattoo can manifest the evolution of a wound—
from dire disfigurement to badge of honor,
for a battle survived, an offense overcome,
an enemy endured.

A wound will take the longest time
before blossoming into its true colors.
And I suspect when I stand before my maker,
they will not look me over for virtues
but will examine me for scars.

And for evidence that I rose above them.

Breakneck

The speed at which no one
would reasonably wish to travel.

Fingertips

Today I saw a good natured young man.
He was blind and his hands were peppered
with scars, hundreds of little cuts and burns—

fingers, knuckles, wrists, palms—
a thousand lessons learned the hard way.
A thousand indignities earned in earnest.

Such are the dangers in daring to reach out.
It occurred to me how often I conceal my own wounds
when this boy seemed to carry his with so little care.

And I thought: what a miracle of connectivity is this skin,
this galaxy of nerve endings we wear so casually,
not so much a patchwork of damage but rather

a history of how we cannot help but to heal,
so much so that I must completely rethink
what it means to hold another's hand.

In Preparation

A narrow band of early light
lay bright across the bedspread,
the only place of color in the room
magnifying the true midnight blue
of his suit slacks and jacket,
an ensemble duly assessed
and laid out with care.
As she would have done.
As she did so many times for him.

Narrow belt, nickel tie clip,
white shirt of just the right tone.
Carefully considered tie—
one of her favorites?
Or perhaps something
more customary to the occasion?
Black is customary.
But black wasn't like her.

She would have stood just so,
shoulders erect, presenting her back,
shifting her hips to step into her heels
while he zipped her up
as he had just days before.
If only he could tie his tie
without her there to straighten it,
without her humming Sinatra,

without the hiss of the iron cooling
as she slipped a newly pressed
handkerchief into his breast pocket.
Now just the tick-tick-tick
of a ceiling fan.
No straightened tie.
No kiss of approval.
No humming.
No hiss. No zip.

My Father in the City of Lights

Paris is portrayed
as a city for lovers.
I went for the first time
with the man I most adore.

He had been many times before
with my mother and was anxious
to show me all the corners
the two of them had loved.

We searched and searched.
And still I loved him all the more
for what he could not find without her.

Ventriloquist

Mouthing the shapes of words while speaking,
is an exercise avoided in earnest
by the fellow with the dummy on his knee.

Sitting in the quiet of my library's reading room
I feel eyes on me—four of them.
Looking up from my book there they are,

an older gentleman, both he
and his painted companion, the same
unblinking expression, heads back, eyes steady,

as though expecting an answer to some unasked question.
I return their gaze, not challenging but curious.
Then one of them speaks:

"You know, you move your lips when you read."
A joggled nod of confirmation from the other.
"It's okay," he confides. *"I do the same thing."*

On the Lake at Dusk
(for George)

My feet out from under me,
I'm flat on the ice
with the clack of my blades on its rock solid surface,
the length of me laid out fully at ease
as though set down at speed but gently so.

How hadn't I noticed these canyons above,
the lovely expanse of sky gaping wide?
Grand maw of the universe, patient, unblinking,
staring down—or benignly staring me down—
twilight bleeding the sky of the last of its blue.

How astounding to meet such comfort
here beneath an indigo cowl of embers,
beacons of travelers in oceans of night.
I am one with… well,…
        … whatever there is to be one with out there.
A moment so magic I dare not compare.

The thunk of a car door from the bridge,
a skittering of footfalls in rapid approach:
"Hey, man, you alright?"
"Just… taking in the stars."
"Oh!" Then with a breathy sigh, *"I thought you—"*

And following my gaze aloft,
the two of us poised on the rim of winter's night,
the silence of a nearby wood our only companion
as the heavens draw a cavernous breath.
And hold it for minutes to come.

Perennial

(for Lynne & Jean Sayles)

The year before he died
my father and I,
on hands and knees,
poked holes in the earth.

Dozens of little graves we dug
along the creek on our property,
into each of which we laid to rest
a handful of little brown bulbs.

Every April now I sit and sun myself
by the quiet water
or stroll among the endless
saffron bursts of daffodils,

straining in their tallness like leggy ballerinas,
radiant perennial reminders
of how the sun still dances
long after it has set.

Acknowledgments

My deep appreciation to friends and enemies who have read, reread and listened to various iterations of many of these pieces—for their gentle opinions and cantankerous rebukes, all of which have made my work better. Sincere thanks to Nora Mossessian and Elaine Bryant, and to the Los Angeles community of writers, workshops and open mics that have permitted me to experiment out loud. Heartfelt gratitude to Lisa Schwarz for her keen eye, kind encouragment and even-keeled cool that kept me from capsizing.

About the Author

Michael J. Cahill was born in Cleveland, Ohio. He has written for radio and for theatre and contributed to independent publications including Wordworth and Nouveau Scarecrow. He lives and writes in North Carolina. *Farewell and Toodle-oo* is his first book of poetry.

9 798224 509751